What people

Kimberly Ivers

cameo portrait of her grandmother, Anne Hunter
Murphy. This little volume reveals the power of
intercessory prayer and it magnifies the importance of
Scripture in shaping lives and providing everyday
guidance. I highly recommend this book to every
person who would like to know Jesus Christ more
personally and to those who are feeling a bit lost and
seeking guidance.

> -Lyle W. Dorsett, PhD, *author, seminary*
> *professor, pastor emeritus Christ the King*
> *Anglican Church, Birmingham AL*

Some of us just survive, some of us thrive, and then
some of us seem to be able to offer help to others, offer
wisdom and strength to buoy others and help them
carry on. Anne Murphy was this type of person. I felt
as I read this book that Kimberly's grandmother was
someone I would truly have loved to have
known. Thankfully through this book I have the
chance to learn about what she gave her family and the
people in her world. I can see why her granddaughter,
Kimberly, felt moved to write this book. Thank you!

> -Jessa Boutte, *business owner, arborist,*
> *working mother, Atlanta, Ga*

Kimberly has documented the timeless wisdom of her
Grandmother Anne along with sharing her own candid
walk with Christ. A refreshing point of view is
presented, as Anne has a wonderfully direct way of
describing her faith, offering compassion and insight
while connecting God's teachings to daily life. Anne

reminded me of my core beliefs as I read this book:
God loves us and we are called to serve Him.

-Brian Bowman, *father, architect, design
director and Professor of Motion Design,
New York, NY*

As I read this book, it was as if my surroundings
melted away and I was transported into Anne
Murphy's living room with Jesus as the host. Reading
about Kimberly's grandmother ushered me back to the
aspirations I had decades ago for my own unhindered
fixation on Him. "Prone to wander and to leave the
God I love", the life of Anne Murphy has invited my
Martha heart to turn once again from the frenzy of self-
reliance to join Mary in sitting quietly and expectantly
at the feet of the Jesus.

-Jane Gilbert, *teacher, writer, community
activist, adoptive mother, Atlanta, GA*

It is as though Kimberly has taken precious pieces of
wisdom passed on from her grandmother and stitched
them together with the loving thread gifted to her in
their tender times together. From it, she has fashioned
a beautiful quilt to wrap us in a hug, not only from her
grandmother, but ultimately from the Lord himself.
We are blessed indeed to have her share this heirloom
with all of us!"

-Jean Jackson, *mother of nine, former
missionary to Japan, grandmother, liaison to
international students within the U.S.
Tacoma, Washington*

One might understandably assume that someone who
lived the preponderance of her life in the 1900's would
have little useful perspective or advice for one deep in

the middle of our high-tech and fast-paced 21st Century. The person with that assumption would be dead wrong. Anne Murphy's faith and wisdom cut right to the heart of what we all need to absorb into our current daily lives. May this book go far to bring a Godly sense of relief to a lot of flailing parents.

-Chuck Johnston, *Founding Headmaster Whitefield Academy, educator, community activist, Atlanta, Ga*

This book is SO good! It was exactly what I needed to read while in the hustle and bustle of life to give me an eternal perspective on all of my daily interactions. I guarantee it will impact its readers for years to come.

-Betsy Jones, *Lead Producer, Professional Voice Over Actor, New York, NY*

As a millennial in America, life can get frustrating and overwhelming with new messages coming from every direction. Heirloom is a little book with a message packed full of beauty and power. As I sat at the feet of Anne Murphy, I felt like I was sitting at the feet of Jesus. And I was. I found myself listening and learning from the rhythms of His life in her. I found myself resting in that timeless and elegantly simple message that Jesus is who He says He is.

-Taylor Pruitt, *Director of Community Engagement, Restore Life, Inc.*

Heirloom

n. something of special value passed
down from one generation to another

The faith and wisdom of Anne Murphy

Written By

Kimberly Iverson

Printed in the United States of America

2018

ISBN 978-1-7263-4486-9

www.journeytoshalom.com
instagram @kimberlyaiverson

Anne Murphy

"Grandma"

Blessed is the one...whose delight is in the law of the Lord, and who meditates on his law day and night. That person is like a tree planted by streams of water, which yields its fruit in season and whose leaf does not wither. Whatever they do prospers.
Psalm 1:1-3

Acknowledgements

I would like to thank my husband, Danny Iverson, who continually loves and supports me in so many ways, including staying up late to help create the book cover and tend to last-minute details. This book could not have been written without you willingly caring for the kids while I escaped to coffee shops to write. You are dearly loved and appreciated, and I couldn't have dreamed up a better husband than you.

A shout out to my kids, Daniel Josiah, Trinity, Katy-Grace, Benjamin, Malachi, Judah, and Gwennalyn, for "sharing mommy" with this call to writing. DJ, KG, and TK, thank you for fixing breakfast and dressing younger siblings on those mornings I was gone. Betsy, thank you for all the encouragement after patiently reading sections and listening to the eternal stream of voice memos that I sent after finishing each section. Jessa Boutte , Eileen Lass and Taylor Pruitt, your editing insights and feedback on this work were of utmost value. Thank you! Erika Collier and Angela Sapp, your prayers sustained and empowered me. I thank the Lord Jesus Christ for the gift of the Holy Spirit who speaks to us, guides us and strengthens us. This book was Your idea in the first place.

~KAI

Dedicated to

*Shashuna, for the years
of watching you persevere,
and always having childlike faith
in the process.*

*And, of course, to Grandma.
Thank you for the precious heirloom
you have given us.
I love you and miss you.
But because of Jesus,
I will see you soon.*

Table of Contents

Forward   14

Introduction   16

    Addendum to the Introduction   18

1. **Eyes that are Good**   24

    Eyes that are Good…in Childhood   26

    Eyes that are Good…Find the Priceless   28

2. **Ears to Hear**   36

    Ears to Hear…Early Tuning   38

    Ears to Hear…Expect to Hear   42

3. **A Posture to Assume**   48

    A Posture of Dependence   49

    A Posture of…Conscious Choosing   53

4. **Habits that Hold**   58

    The Habit of Good Habits   59

    The Habit of Availability   62

    The Habit of Reflection   63

    The Habit of Yielding   65

5. **A Message to Share**   68

    God, a Storyteller   71

    A Message to Mothers   75

    Just Brag on Jesus   78

6. **Conclusion**   86

~Forward~

I spent a good deal of yesterday reading Kimberly's book, and it's so good I can hardly stand it. I loved the book! I already knew Kimberly was a gifted writer, but this is more than gifted writing. It has a supernatural quality to it that "smells like Jesus."

And she preached the Gospel to me! As you know, I'm a cynical old preacher who has to see the real deal sometimes just to keep from being a Buddhist. Kimberly and Danny Iverson have always been that to me… and now Anne Murphy is too.

~~~

It happens rarely, but sometimes a book comes along that is so refreshing, so honest and so real that you want everybody you know to read it. *Heirloom* is about the author's grandmother, Anne Murphy, but it's not what you think. It's really about Jesus. When I finished reading the book I realized what an attraction Anne Murphy adds to heaven; I was blessed with the freshness, the authenticity of and the gifted writing of the author. But more than that, I "heard the soft sound of sandaled feet" on every page. It's about Jesus, his unconditional love and grace, and his faithfulness. Read this book. You'll laugh, cry… and worship. Then you'll give it to everyone you know.

-Dr. Steve Brown
Author, broadcaster, seminary professor, founder and president of Key Life Network, Orlando, Fl.

~ Introduction~

February 2018

Why write a book about *my* grandmother? Why would anyone else be interested?

I am a motherless mother. But I am not a grandmother-less mother. By the tender age of twenty, cancer had worked its cruel fate on my mother, plus three grandparents. Because of this last remaining "grand" in my life, I still have a wealth of wisdom, a treasury of knowledge, a fountain of encouragement and a supply of support.

Shashuna is a motherless mother as well. But she is also a fatherless, aunt-less, uncle-less, grandfather-less and grandmother-less mother. All taken from her by the streets of inner city Newark, NJ, alcoholism, drugs or jail, she lost them early in life. Her grandmother, who raised her in her mother's absence, died when Shashuna was in the throes of having and raising her own kids. In knowing her, and the many other amazingly strong women I have met throughout years of inner city life, I have humbly realized the incredible privilege it is to call Anne Murphy "Grandma"- a privilege I do not want to take for granted. Recording her wisdom is an attempt to make "Grandma" accessible to the "Shashunas" of the world.

Whether your story is blessed and privileged to have known older, wiser counselors throughout it or if your story has known loss and want of such supports, I write this Heirloom for you. Each of us needs a wise, encouraging, supportive grandma to help us get back up when we fall down, realign us when we get off track, and encourage us when we feel defeated. And, of course, Grandma's guidance might just keep us from landing in those places in the first place…. or at least, maybe, a little less frequently.

If you are one of "us" then, welcome. Grab a cup of coffee. Imagine yourself on Grandma's floral antique love seat with walls of family pictures enclosing you into a sense of belonging and connection, for connected you are. Our Elder Brother (Hebrews 2:11, Mark 3:34) and Savior (Luke 2:11, 1 Timothy 1:15) has paid for your spot in the family- a family where love flourishes, Truth resounds, the Spirit comforts, and the Father welcomes. He has sent grandmas like mine to communicate who He is and just how much He wants you welcomed in.

Addendum to the Introduction

August 2018

The previous introduction was written in the early spring of 2018. I didn't know all would change so quickly. I *did* know the Spirit's nudging, and *He* knew what He was doing….

The year 2018 greeted me with grief. The same exact type of brain tumor which slowly robbed me of my mother and took her life when I was 15 years old, did so for my uncle in January. It was as if suddenly the 20-year interim between deaths never occurred and I was transported to my hurting, raw teenage self with all the pain and loss and wrestling to deal with. My Grandma was now reliving the grief as well, having now lost two children in this heart wrenching manner. A month later, Grandma's brother, her across the street neighbor and old-age companion, passed away suddenly. A multileveled grief ensued. There was now grieving over suppressed loss from mother-void, grieving over uncle and great-uncle, and grieving for Grandma, who at the ripe age of 92 should have been spared, in my humble opinion, any more loss. Many a phone call connected us as we processed these losses and mutually shared how the Scriptures spoke to us in our pain. Our hearts were further intertwined and comforted in our Lord Jesus who Himself was well acquainted with grief (Isaiah 53:3).

~~~~

Tuesday afternoons were our "entering in" that we did, myself and two other moms, as we poured out our hearts, poured out our praise, and poured out ourselves before the Lord together. As we gathered that chilly February afternoon, I couldn't get through our initial conversation without getting choked up, tears involuntarily spilling down my cheeks. They pried, and I shared the loss, as well as the experience of processing it all with my wise, loving Grandmother, who had even deeper grief to bear than my own.

"Wow, what I would give to be able to sit down and ask your grandmother a few things. I've never had a real relationship with my grandmother, much less a godly one," were their responses.

And we proceeded to pray.

Intercessions commenced, and tears were shed, and praise was given, and it was during this time that I saw a picture of a book, like a journal with the words, "My Heirloom" on it. Suddenly the Spirit of God burned in me the need to capture this gem of a woman that I was privileged to call "Grandma." I knew exactly what I needed to do—set about recording her thoughts, wise sayings, and insights from the Word into a journal-like composition so that I could share it with her family and particularly her great-grandchildren (seven of whom I was raising). It was an honor to have her, one I often took for granted; and documenting who she was and what she thought and said would be a gift to myself, her extended family and possibly others who never knew what it was like to have a constant prayer warrior, a listening ear and an always-wise counselor. My own children, who enjoyed frequenting her home, playing with her toys and partaking of her homemade Blethemhouse cookies, might not think to ask those questions which would result in time-tried counsel that would support them through hardships in life. ("Grandma, may I have another cookie?" might not help them when they are married and raising their own children.)

After our prayer time, I actually googled the word "heirloom" because I needed a refresher on what the true definition was. Upon reading it, I knew this was from the Lord.

Heirloom-n. something of special value handed down from one generation to another.

Nothing could be of greater value to pass down from one generation to the next than Grandma's faith and humble walk with the Lord. And now, the Lord had prompted me to begin preserving it through writing it out.

~~~~

I obeyed the prompting.

I can't always claim prompt obedience, but this time I did.

I began calling Grandma more frequently with pen in ready position over notebook in order to document our conversations and record the wisdom she shared. I brainstormed questions to ask her, ones to which I would want my children to know the answers. I made intentional trips to Birmingham to see her and overlapped them with her Tuesday morning Bible study. I utilized voice memo on my iPhone to record conversations, whether they were about Scripture she read or the mother goose we observed caring for her eggs at the nearby Aldridge Gardens during our stroll around the lake. I savored and soaked in each interaction, because I needed to collect it for this writing endeavor. I was doing the work of a curator, preserving this precious heirloom to be passed on.

The Lord could not have been more kind or gentle to me with my beloved grandmother's departure from this world. He knew the pain and He knew the void it would leave, but He allowed me to fine-tune my focus on her right before a massive stroke would paralyze her left side, rendering her unable to speak to me during the last few days I would spend with her in this life. The Lord would ease me into the loss of her physical presence with me, for the Spirit's instructions were to journal our conversations rather than type them. As soon as I was notified of her stroke (while I was on a trip in Norway), I busily began typing out our conversations and our last experiences together. My last days with her I read aloud the beginnings of this tribute, as an offering of thanks for all she had imparted. In the days and weeks after her death, she was still with me, her voice still in my ear, her thoughts still pondered over, as I pieced together those conversations that I had been able to have with her before she was gone.

The following is the preservation of some of those final thoughts, words of wisdom and Scriptural insight passed down in the last six months of this amazing woman's life.

~1~

Eyes that are Good

"The eye is the lamp of the body. So, if your eye is healthy, your whole body will be full of light." Matthew 6:22

Hers were good. Really good. Every time I talked on the phone with her, she would share about the good in her life. Her good, healthy eyes had been trained, disciplined to see correctly into each and every situation. Never mind the fact that she had just lost her son to the same exact brain cancer that took her daughter twenty years earlier. Never mind that her brother and old-age companion passed away suddenly just weeks after losing her son, thus leaving a double void in her life. Never mind the fact that she was nearly 93 and she still had a revolving door of a household with people constantly coming through to stay with her, pop in to visit her, or settle in to learn from one of her weekly Bible studies. She always spoke of God's faithfulness. "The Lord is just so good," she would say, and then proceed to name tiny graces He had given, or glimpses into His Word that He had bestowed, or relationships that had come to enrich her life. She was choosing to give thanks that her life was so full. She could have easily complained about how many guests (both invited and *uninvited*) graced her doorstep. But because she knew the love of God and knew His love for His people, she welcomed each one.

How does one learn to see, name and receive fullness from all the good? How does one do it when much around you seems bad?

"I lift up my eyes to You, to You who sit enthroned in heaven" Psalm 123:1 (NIV)

It seems that her eyes were continually being lifted up, and it was in that upward gaze that she could see a good and faithful King on His throne. He was seated on it, established, so all below was under His Lordship and reign. For this very reason, all could be counted as good.

The ability to see the good in every situation started at a young age for Grandma. But it was also tested at a young age. Her spiritual vision that could pierce through the cloudiest of situations to see the blessings in them was not just a natural inclination, but an exercise of the will. How can one learn to continually find the good, even in the fiercest of life's storms?

In 92 years of life, this woman, Anne Murphy, modeled how.

Eyes that are Good...in Childhood

"Family relationships and childhood experiences are our first teachers, and often the first means by which we begin to be aware of God and hear Him "speak" to us.

Our interpretation of these things plays a role in the shaping of our adult life."

-Anne Murphy
This I Know

Grandma's view of the world being so good was cultivated early in her childhood, as she recounted all the blessings in her life and observed the wonder of God's creation. She relates a story in her book, This I Know, of such a view.

"The back bedroom was large and airy, with open windows on two sides. I was lying on the bed, on my stomach with my elbows propping my chin in my hands, musing about all the things I liked in my eight-year-old life. Thinking no one could hear me, I began singing a little song of praise to God. 'Father, I love you. You are so good to me — I thank You for all the nice things You give me.' I paused to think of some of the specifics I'd like to mention, when to my utter surprise and horror, Papa [her father] stepped into the room smiling, and said, 'Why, what a sweet song! Thank you, honey!', I was stricken. He thought I was singing about him! Too embarrassed to correct his mistake, I slid off the bed and took his hand. We walked together out of the room." (This I Know, p.7)

And then again, she reflects on how happy and pleasant things were, as she gazed upon the beauty, stillness and splendor of God's creation.

"I can't consciously remember my parents or adult relatives talking to me about God, or how they felt about Him…. But I remember waking up summer mornings on the sleeping porch and lying in bed watching the daylight break through the leaves of the pecan tree that shaded the porch. I remember listening to the birds and thinking about how nice it was to be out of school for the summer. I remember feeling so free and happy that it seemed natural and sensible to thank God for all the things I loved. I'd not yet read *Psalm 66:3*, but I was in agreement with it — *'Say to God, how awesome are Your works!'"* (<u>This I Know</u>, p.10)

I can't help but think about every home that Grandma has had. There was a continual endeavor to plant new plants everywhere she lived, whether she had a large space or a tiny one. Maybe not with the greenest of thumbs did she cultivate all those plants (quite a few died along the way) but she relished the ones that survived. Quite possibly this was a continual "returning" to the ways that God first captivated her eyes and attention to the fact that *He is good*. He has manifested His goodness in every plant, every bird song, every refreshing breeze, every ray of sunshine "breaking through the leaves." Just as she cultivated the plants and flowers that spoke of His goodness, she also cultivated a view of the best all throughout her life.

Eyes that are Good...Find the Priceless and Invest in it.

"Don't store up treasures here on earth, where moths eat them and rust destroys them, and where thieves break in and steal. Store your treasures in heaven, where moths and rust cannot destroy, and thieves do not break in and steal. Wherever your treasure is, there the desires of your heart will also be." Matthew 6:19-21 (NLT)

"I'd love for you to come see me again, honey."

She had just finished catching me up to speed on what she had been doing the past couple of weeks. It was mid-June and it sounded more like the schedule of a booming "Anne's Bed and Breakfast" than the schedule of an almost 93-year-old. The visitors were constant.

"Grandma! Aren't you worn out? I want to get over there, but I don't want to overwhelm you with constant visitors!"

Her response…

"I am fully aware that, being in my nineties, I am in the final chapter of my life, and so I welcome all the people I can see while I can see them. I want to enjoy them while I am still here. "(June 6, 2018)

Her response and my assumption juxtaposed two different world views.

My assumption reflected a view that people are a burden and add stress and chaos to your life, and possibly get in the way of what you actually want to be doing. Grandma's outlook was that people, especially family members, added a richness and depth to one's life, and there is no greater priority (besides spending time with the Lord) than knowing and treasuring those relationships which God has entrusted to us.

Conversations we had in the past reverberated from the memories…

"My family is one of my greatest treasures in this life, they are such a gift from God. You know, in Genesis, the very first thing God established after He created the world, was the institution of the family. If God made that a priority and the very first building block of humanity, then I think it would be a wise investment for us to do the same. "

I tune back in to the conversation at hand…

"God is just too good for us to focus on what we *don't* have. So, I want to see all the people I *do* have."

I could sense a preaching to oneself or reiterating what the Lord had been impressing on her heart, probably in those long quiet times as she grieved the recent loss of her son and brother, to add to the many whom she had already said goodbye to. In the past 20 years she had experienced a sort of wiping out of her generation and all those she held dear from years past. She could easily have allowed the grief and loss to consume her.

"We get to choose what we see and invest in. When the Israelites were in the desert, the ones that complained and doubted the goodness of God ended up dying in the dry and bleak wilderness. They made a rather unwise investment, I have observed."

Grandma never lost her ability to interject her witty sarcasm into even the deepest of theological concepts.

"The ones that stayed alive were the ones that learned complete dependence upon the Lord for everything, trusting that He was doing good for them. Because of their dependence on Him they were guided in how to move out of the desert and into the promised land. When they were constantly seeking the Lord and moving at His command, they were able to overcome and defeat overwhelming enemies along the way."(Joshua 5:6,7,9; Numbers 14:2 and 32:11-13)

The conversation was then interrupted by some sort of child's urgent need and thus ended quickly. But this was not the only time that month that she asked for me to come see her. It was as if she knew that the end was drawing near.

I did come see her.

But it was *after* she suffered a major stroke.

I came and saw her in the heat of early July and sat with her and sang to her and read Scripture to her and prayed with her on her last few days on earth. She was no longer able to speak, but she had used her words wisely when she was able, so they were enough. Enough to fill a soul, and renew a mind, and refocus one's sight. Now it was my turn to affirm and encourage and speak life into her.

~~~~~

Grandma went to be with Jesus this past week (July 11, 2018). Hers was one of the human relationships I have treasured most deeply out of all the fleeting "treasures" of this life. The treasure trove of "Grandma" was enjoyed through talking and listening, just sitting and sipping coffee, and reflecting on and reading Scripture. Two hearts were deeply intertwined because of a mutual love for the Lord and for each other. We had truly treasured. We had treasured each other.

I headed home after a week of continual tears and gut-wrenching loss as we watched Grandma deteriorate quickly after her stroke. It left an utter void as I departed from Grandma's haven-home that had now turned empty. I returned to a home brimming with life — a husband to hold and walk alongside. Seven unique individuals growing, ever needing someone to listen to them, guide them, and support them as they navigate all the pressing concerns of their ever-widening little worlds.

As if that were not enough life, there was the teenage boy from our neighborhood living with us for the summer since his family got evicted. Then also the the family of five that had moved in for two weeks to give them a break from forking out the exorbitant cost of "a week by week roof over our heads" in the form of an extended-stay hotel. On top of that there are the many neighborhood kids who know that "there's always a party at the Iversons!" so they come by to hang out.

I can almost hear Grandma's words and her hearty chuckle at the various adventures I often (but not this time) reported to her throughout the years of living and serving in the inner city,

"Well, honey, you indeed have a full life. At least you aren't bored!"

At least *someone* could laugh about it!

I, on the other hand, could so easily get overwhelmed about it all and look right past the *people* that all this activity represents and just see the laundry scattered and ever-accumulating, more mouths to be fed, more dishes to be cleaned up, more noise to endure, more bodies to be directed and more to-do list items that just don't get done because new ones have emerged with the crowd.

Or…

I could look upon it all with "eyes that are good" and choose to see it all differently. All of the activity could mean more relationships to be enjoyed, which is what Grandma so often saw. Along with the whirlwind and the ensuing disheveled house, there's *more* - more conversations to be had, more smiles to be shared, more hearts to be poured out, more prayers to be prayed, more creativity to be inspired, and more lives to be intertwined. It takes good eyes to *see* all this and an eternally-minded heart to *invest* in it all. Small sacrifices made with the joy and the strength of the Lord become an eternal investment which accumulates great wealth. It is an inheritance stored up in *people* over places and *persons* over their performance.

Grandma had chosen the former, and because of that, she died one of the richest women on earth. A multitude of souls she had invested in awaited her in heaven, and a multitude mourned her leaving. She had truly stored up her treasures in heaven. One day her deposits on both sides of glory will all be joined together in the presence of the Lord she served and the God of love she lived for.

~2~

Ears to Hear

I was eight years old when the mind-numbing reality was told to me.

I had been reflecting on a recent Sunday School lesson about God speaking to Moses in the burning bush and posed my ponderings to my mother.

"Why doesn't God speak to people like He used to in the Bible?"

"He does, Kimberly. He has given us the Bible and speaks to us through it. Also, He speaks to people now sometimes too."

Then she hit me with it, leaving me dumbfounded.

"Grandma hears God speak."

"Wait. Grandma? MY Grandma? Grandma can HEAR God? Like, she has heard His voice?"

My brain swirled with this possibility, especially in light of the fact that much of what I had known of God was through felt board Sunday School lessons and kids Bible videos. (I also knew for a fact that God helped people find their car keys, because He had done it for my mom…on numerous occasions.)

Could God really be that personal?

Suddenly, the far-off and somewhat impersonal God I knew of through Bible stories seemed closer. If the Grandma that I loved, the one that gave back-scratches and baked cookies and served tea biscuits could hear Him speak, then maybe He wasn't so distant after all. Expectation shifted in my young eight-year-old mind.

Years would pass, and my own faith would grow, and habits of reading the Scriptures and prayer would develop and trials would be faced, and my own listening ear would be tuned. I would come to know that Jesus' death and resurrection enabled us to be adopted into His Father's family. I would experience the Holy Spirit as a Person empowering us to stay connected *to* our Father. I would begin to hear the Father's voice. I would sample what joy could be experienced in those times of being so deeply impressed by God's Spirit that it really felt like His voice burning it in my spirit.

But Grandma? Her "hearing" was a daily one. Maybe even hourly.

God spoke.

Grandma listened.

Because she had ears to hear.

Ears to Hear...Early Tuning

"Grandma, how did you get so good at hearing God's voice?"

Kids were in bed at a decent time. (which is nothing short of a miracle, because with seven children, bedtime can be an upwards-of-two-hour-long crisis. Every. Single. Night.) I knew that the only way I'd have the time to call Grandma, interview her and write about the heirloom of her faith, was if I was doggedly strategic and motivated to shave off the extra hour of crisis diversions so that all energetic and manipulating little beings were in bed by 8:15. On this early-March evening at least I still had Daylight Savings Time working in my favor.

"Well, honey, it actually started a lot like what we're doing right now. Granddaddy would be off working at the nightclubs, and my little ones would be asleep (hers, I'm sure, went to bed angelically and never put up a fuss) so I'd lie there in bed and just talk to God about things. He was a very good listener. When I realized how little I knew of all that He wanted to say back to me (in the Bible) I started reading the Scriptures as well. It really is amazing how willing God is to speak to us, if we are just willing to hear what He has to say."

She then began to digress into a remembrance.

"You know, a memory from when I was just about three or four years old popped up in my mind the other day. It seemed so…. random, but I might as well share it with you…

"My mama had taken me to church and she was walking me to my Sunday School classroom. It was a really old building, and my classroom happened to be up a very steep winding stairwell. I just remember hanging on so tightly to the rail on one side, and Mama was holding my hand on the other side. I was so frightened, and it seemed to take such a long time to get up there. I really was hanging on for dear life (or so I thought). I remember finally getting to the top of the stairs, where my Sunday School teacher, who was...well, I'll refrain from using the word 'fat', but pleasantly rotund, came up and stooped down and hugged me and exclaimed,

'Oh! I'm so glad you made it. You are just so brave to have come up all those steep, steep steps.'

"I remember being so thankful that she noticed all the treachery I had endured to get up to that class. It was so comforting to feel known by her.

"As, I look back, I think God was using her, at that young age in my life, to speak to me, to let me know that **the Lord** *knows* **us,** *sees* **what we are going through and** *wants* **to comfort us.**

"I am just amazed that I still had that memory, ninety years later."

As I listened to this story, and the enduring lesson that Grandma learned from it, one that would mark her life full of grief and loss, I suddenly loved this rotund Sunday School teacher. Her elderly, stout self who chose to welcome little Anne with a giant hug and affirmation for having braved a long steep flight of steps with miniature legs and feet, engaged in an act that would be paid forward thousandfold through that little Anne grown big. Little did she know that by simply showing up that morning, by simply volunteering to take on the young class, by choosing to see a small child and welcome them with warm embrace, she was fulfilling Jesus's promise, *"And anyone who welcomes a little child like this on My behalf* **is welcoming Me.**" (Matthew 18:5, NLT)

Jesus was truly welcomed into that moment. For in that act of the Sunday School teacher welcoming Anne, Jesus was welcomed into Anne's heart and life and memory. That memory lasted nine decades, nearly a century, and it left a message from the Lord, in a form that a young child could understand. "I see you. I know you. I welcome you. I comfort you."

Jesus would go on to tell Anne these same words through many different life seasons and struggles. He would use many different means: promises in His Word, worship and prayer in the local church, circumstances, and individuals obeying the prompting of the Holy Spirit. But for this young age, and these not-yet-tuned ears, He spoke in a way that He could be heard.

And isn't that what He wants to do for all of us?

Isn't it what Grandma would want for all of us?

Ears to Hear...*Expect* to Hear

Grandma's greatest wisdom was that she knew she didn't have the wisdom.

But she knew where to find it.

All those who knew her subconsciously lived with the belief that Grandma would always have the answer. This was exactly why hers was the number dialed after sleepless nights of deliberating over an agonizing (or seemingly so) dilemma.

"Anne will know what to do."

And she did.

Not that she had memorized the answer to every problem of the twenty-first century, but she knew where to go to hear the answer. And she so gracefully and articulately led us there.

~~~~

I would call her up with head all jumbled as I wrestled through a decision or grappled with the hard parts of life. As I spewed my plight, she would so patiently listen. She would humbly entertain all my well-worried-over angles on a situation or the circular thinking that got me into this stressed-out mess in the first place. And when I was finally finished, she would say,

"Well, honey, I don't know what you are supposed to do, but Jesus does. Let's go to Him and ask Him. "

It was exasperating. And empowering. At the same time. She wasn't discounting the dilemma or even my angst, and she wasn't even telling me something I didn't already *know*. It's just that I had been so busy focusing on the dilemma (and getting my panties in a wad in the process) that I forgot the simple truth so plainly before me. **Jesus always has the answer.**

Grandma's advice wasn't something new, but something *forgotten*. And often, she would then lead me into the Presence of the One who can calm every fear, direct every stumbling foot, strengthen every weak knee.

She would proceed to pray....

"Lord Jesus..."

So quietly and gently.

What proceeded was not some desperate pleading and crying out, nor was it some loud declaration of our limited perspective, "We now declare and decree that

Kimberly will know what to do!!! We command every obstacle to leave!!!"

No, when we would pray, her voice would get so low and quiet that my ears would have to strain to hear her. It was as if she was just speaking to Someone so deeply imbedded *in* her, and so *near* to her that I, as an outsider, would need to perk up and sidle up just to be able to hear. This was an intimate communion that had been cultivated for years through those daily morning times with Bible open in lap, journal spread out, and prayers being lifted. This was an insider's conversation.

"Come, Holy Spirit."

She would continue with such affection and familiarity.

"You know how much we need You. We thank You that You are here with us…"

And she would proceed to lay out our desire for wisdom and direction and just trail off into the stillness. The stillness of expectation. Expectation that the Holy Spirit, as a Person, was there with us and would be doing what the Lord Jesus had told us He would do: comfort, lead into all truth, and empower us (John 14:16-18; John 16:13, Acts 1:8).

One of the most exasperating, but empowering pieces of advice she gave wasn't really advice, but a **setting of expectation.**

In the Scriptures, it was this type of *expectation* which preceded the moving of our Lord, the hearing of His voice, the witnessing of Jesus' miracles.

One of the first people in the New Testament to experience Jesus after years of expectation was Anna, the elderly Jewish woman who greeted the Messiah at the time of Jesus' dedication. She had lived long, prayed and fasted long, and waited long in expectation for this coming One. When He was eight days old and presented in the temple, she was able to experience *in reality* the Savior sent by the One she had so often prayed to, listened for and spoke on behalf of (Luke 2:36-38).

Later, Jesus grew older and began His earthly ministry of healing and speaking. It was those who truly believed that He was not only ABLE, but WILLING to meet them in their need that got to experience His miraculous touch.

The outcast leper declared such expectancy when he approached Jesus. He walked away with his hopes realized.

"'If You will, You can make me clean.' Moved with pity, He [Jesus] stretched out his hand and touched him and said to him, 'I will; be clean.' And immediately the leprosy left him, and he was made clean." Mark 1:40-41

Jesus delighted to heal the centurion's servant when he communicated such faith and expectation in Jesus' ability and authority....

"'But say the word and let my servant be healed...' When Jesus heard these things, He marveled at him, and turning to the crowd that followed Him, said, 'I tell you, not even in Israel have I found such faith.' And when those who had been sent returned to the house, they found the servant well." Luke 7:7-10

And those that didn't expect much? They didn't receive much.

"Is this not the carpenter's son? ...And He did not do many mighty works there, because of their unbelief." Matthew 13:55, 58

Grandma had learned this lesson of expectation early on- that Jesus was absolutely trustworthy. He was willing. He was able. And that God loved to speak to His children. Hers were the ears that were ready in anticipation for the Spirit's promptings. Hers was the life lived in prompt obedience. Hers was the heart that felt the Lord's Presence so intimately. Because of this, any of us needing help or clarity knew exactly where to go to help us remember how to hear again.

~3~

A Posture to Assume

In every picture, she was the slim delicate figure poised with erect posture next to her tall, burly husband. Her slight frame could be deceptive, for it housed a powerhouse of a woman. Who knew that a woman who looked so frail at times, would be one who moved mountains on her knees? She always stood aright, never leaning, never slouching, and her outward countenance exhibited the position of her heart. Psalm 11:7 states,

"For the LORD is righteous, He loves righteousness;
the upright will behold His face."

Grandma walked uprightly with her God, thus placing her whole being in a position which allowed for a continual filling, empowering, and beholding. Hers was a posture which caused her to be an easily-filled vessel. Hers was a posture to be assumed.

A Posture of Dependence

"Because I need Him so much"
                              -Anne Murphy, AD 2018

"O God, you are my God; earnestly I seek you; my soul thirst for you; my flesh faints for you, as in a dry and weary land where there is no water." Psalm 63:1
                              -David, King of Israel, 1000 BC

Grandma was sitting in her "quiet time chair" in her living room. The one that was home to "Baxter's Pillow" when she herself was not occupying it with Bible in lap and reference books and devotionals placed around her on varying side tables. We had just finished reviewing our morning's quiet times. I'm pretty sure what I had gleaned from the Word and shared was a fumbling, "I really need to stop yelling at my kids so much."

Her gleaning?

A rich overflow of wisdom, affirmation and encouragement with each word that she read popping out of the pages and speaking to different situations in her life and mine. It felt as if I had just feasted on the richest of foods (which, of course, I had). I pushed back from the "meal," satisfied and in awe.

"Grandma, how are you able to glean so much from the Scriptures? Everything just pops out to you and applies immediately to what we're going through. You're so diligent about having long quiet times and not getting distracted with other things. How do you do it?"

Grandma gently replied,

"You know, other people have asked me about that. It's really not that I'm so special. I just don't think they realize…

"I spend so much time with the Lord in the Scriptures…"

And I wait for the hidden secret of this amazingly strong, godly woman, who has stood the test of decades of joys and sorrows, victories and trials, and continues to walk with her God and serve Him with faithfulness.

"I spend so much time with Him…because I need Him so much."

There it was. Need.

The secret of this woman to whom so many went to for strength: need.

We all have it. We are all a desperate bunch. We can take our need and run to all the people around us, or to frantic activity, or to fleeting experiences, or to temporary substances to try to meet that need.

Or.

We can bring our need to the One who "fills all things everywhere with Himself" (Ephesians 1:23).

Which is what Grandma did, thus placing herself in a continual posture of dependence upon the Lord for every detail of her life.

There was a constant strength in her, a constant eye for seeing the good, a constant ear for hearing the Lord's voice, all because of this constant dependence upon Him. Her strength came from a continual drawing from the mighty God who breathed His breath into her each morning. She joined the saints of ages past who *waited for the Lord more than watchmen waited for the morning. Her whole being waited for Him, and she hoped in His Word continually.* (Psalm 130:5-6) She longed for *Him*, not just what He could give.

She didn't study those Scriptures just to have an amazing Bible study to teach to the women who flocked to her. She did not fall into the trap of the "religious folk" of Jesus' day, who studied the Scriptures diligently because they thought that in *them* they had eternal life (John 5:39). No, she realized that they were the very Scriptures that testified about Jesus Christ, the Messiah, and she did not refuse to come to *Him* to have life. It became the posture she assumed: living *in* Him, and living *out* of His promise in John 16:33, "*I have told you these things, so that in Me you may have peace.*"

Grandma's quiet times were driven by **need**,

and her life was lived in a posture of **dependence,**

on a Person who promised a **filling**

of **power** and **peace**

through the gift of the **Holy Spirit.**

Her **need** became her greatest **Strength**.

A Posture of...Conscious Choosing

"But if you refuse to serve the Lord,
choose today whom you will serve…
But as for me and my family, we will serve the Lord."
Joshua 24:15

A long letter I had written to Grandma was sitting open in her lap. The April sun beat down upon the pretty planted pansies, as well as on us, while we sat upon the back patio. The back patio did not overlook a lush farm or shimmering lake (Grandma's life wasn't *that* quintessential), but rather we were framed by different pots of flowers and small shrubs which Grandma had planted to bring beauty to an otherwise small, bland space. A movie played on Grandma's computer, and small children were huddled on the side of her bed in order to watch. Yes, ninety-two-year-old Grandma had learned how to utilize technology as its newness came barreling towards her. We were managing to steal a chunk of time in order to sit and chat. She was about to "tend to" the many laments and thoughts poured out in my letter.

Her gentle scratchy southern drawl began.

"We are often choosing, honey. Life is a choice. We are choosing what we think about. Because we get to decide what we will think upon, we're ultimately choosing our attitude — choosing joy and gratitude or choosing to look at the negative and complain.

"When I was raising our five kids and started to get overwhelmed by the responsibilities of it all, sometimes I would just have to remind myself: I chose this. I chose to get married to Granddaddy. I chose to do it young. I chose to have a big family. God wants us to have joy in the choices we've made. We can see what is here and now and choose to say, 'Thank You, Lord,' for the good in it. Then we can relax into our lives and simply receive the gift that it is.

"I know it's easy to get overwhelmed, honey. When I could feel myself getting overwhelmed by my schedule, I knew that if I just focused on the blessings in the midst of it all, it would help my overall attitude. When everything seemed to bombard me, I would have to tell myself, 'I might not be able to get everything under control, but I can at least do this one little thing.' I would set my mind to getting that task done, and then I would move on to the next thing. I found that even in this little 'trick,' I was choosing whether or not to get overwhelmed.

"You know, we can also be our own worst enemy. We can choose to criticize and complain about everything around us, or even the things *in* us that we don't like. That can drain *any* possibility of joy out of just about any situation we find ourselves in. We also get to choose if we will allow fear to creep in and steal our peace. We get to choose if we will let worry divert us from the present, which would keep us from fully relishing the moment and entering into it. Worry is just rushing ahead mentally. These kinds of mindsets that mar our happiness and joy can lead us into a "just enduring" state. If we aren't careful, we let the overwhelming and hard things bury all the smaller joys and blessings.

"Trust, though, is the opposite of this. It is knowing that the circumstance God has us in is His good pleasure and we just say, 'Thank You'. You know, so many women my, ahem, rather ripe age (spoken with Grandma's typical tongue-in-cheek sarcasm), or even younger, have aches and pains that plague them. Every morning I wake up and just say 'Thank You' for the fact that nothing hurts right now. It is such a gift. It could be easy to overlook if I am not choosing to think about all the wonderful gifts God *has* given me.

"I think it boils down to what God laid out for us there in Deuteronomy, when He said,

> *'Today I have given you the choice between life and death, between blessings and curses. Now I call on heaven and earth to witness the choice you make.*
> *Oh, that you would choose life,*
> *so that you and your offspring (family) might live!'*
> *(Deuteronomy 30:19 NLT)*

"When God created man, He gave us stewardship-stewardship over ourselves, over creation, over our families. Our thoughts and habits and emotions are all part of that as well. We get to choose life and death when we get to choose our thoughts…."

And I realized it, there, sitting in the sun on Grandma's peaceful patio.

Grandma's full and fruitful life did not occur by mere happenstance. Ninety-two years of health and service, and love and discipleship were just a crowning representation of hundreds, even thousands, of tiny *choices*. Grandma had done a lot of choosing in her life. She chose to own all the circumstances she found herself in, the people she found herself amongst, and the experiences she lived out. Her choosing to receive it all, her choosing to give thanks in it all, her choosing to trust the Lord in it all, was a choice that not only brought *her* life, but brought life to her offspring as well. It was just as God promised in Deuteronomy: "*Choose life, so that you and your offspring might live!*" Her "offspring" actually far surpassed her five biological children, sixteen grandchildren and twenty great-grandchildren. Because of her willingness to serve the Lord wherever He placed her, she had acquired many more spiritual offspring throughout the years. Individuals who had sought her counsel and her wisdom from the Scriptures, even those who are reading her counsel right now continue to gain from her tiny choices made in light of the goodness of God and His faithfulness to His Word.

~ 4 ~

Habits that Hold

I had pulled away from a busy life with seven kids' different schedules in Atlanta in order to come see her. I came to experience what other women, strangers to me, adored her for.

Her Bible studies.

I, as her granddaughter, received her wisdom by osmosis through our conversations about our lives and through her ever-faithful letter-writing. These women, though, gathered in her home weekly to sit at the feet of Anne and glean from what she had absorbed as she daily sat at the feet of Jesus.

Line by line, week by week, they read through different books of the Bible. What emerged was a graceful intermingling of Biblical knowledge, 90 years of life experience, whisperings heard from listening long in the presence of God — all funneled into intensely practical ways of applying and believing the Scriptures in real life.

No wonder women throughout all the stages of Grandma's life had gathered around her to glean from her wisdom!

And now, on this April morning, I was counted in their number.

We sat around the table and opened our Bibles up to Mark 12. No coffee or tea was served because each woman anticipated a far better refreshment...

the voice of God speaking through His Word...
and speaking through Anne.

The Habit of Good Habits

Grandma opened our time in prayer, just gently and humbly inviting the Holy Spirit into our midst in order for us to hear Him speak through the Scriptures. We then proceeded to read through the passage with Grandma, intermittently stopping to expound on phrases and verses.

"Jesus then began to speak to them in parables: 'A man planted a vineyard. He put a wall around it, dug a pit for the winepress and built a watchtower. Then he rented the vineyard to some farmers and moved to another place. At harvest time he sent a servant to the tenants to collect from them some of the fruit of the vineyard."
Mark 12:1-3 (NIV)

Grandma began.

"The man in this story built a vineyard and then leased it out. He created it and then entrusted it. He gave stewardship to the men he left it with in order for them to use it and to produce something with it. God has done the same with us as His creation. He made us and then allows us to be stewards of our lives. Being a steward of our lives is a fancy way of saying, 'God gave us a brain, and He actually wants us to use it!'"

She spoke it as an aside and offered such obvious but sometimes hidden practical advice which could be put to use…. immediately.

"The man planted a vineyard just as God has planted the seed of the Holy Spirit in us. The man put a wall up around the vineyard and similarly God provides a protection around us so that the seed of His Word and His Presence can be shielded from the evil one. We don't have to worry. If we are His vineyard then that protection is there whether we are conscious of it or not. If we believe that God has planted a wall around us, then with whatever enters into our lives we can trust that God has allowed its entrance for a reason. Another wall around us that can protect and provide boundaries are the habits we form. They can often shield us and keep us in place no matter what we might be reeling from in the hard knocks of life."

"You know, it has been so hard…"

Her voice started to quiver as emotion welled up. The deep sorrow she carried broke through the steadfast woman we all saw…

"Losing my brother Billy and his companionship as we have lived these later widowed years across the street from each other has left such a huge void. I used to go over and spend time with him every day, but now, I'll suddenly remember that I can't do that anymore, and it feels like 'Now what?' On top of that, having lost him so close to losing my son, Chuck, to cancer last month…."

Tears fell, and through choked voice...

"…it would be quite easy to just let all the sorrow bury you into not wanting to do *anything*."

Composure was resumed, and she continued...

"This is where the importance of habits is found. The habits that I had before all this grief hit have proven to be like walls. They are like the walls around the vineyard, giving guidance and boundaries and protection in times when outside dangers threaten us. Instead of sitting around thinking about how devastating all this is when the waves of grief and the 'Now what?' encroaches, I just tell myself, 'Do as you have always done.' Before both Chuck and Billy died, I always got up, had my quiet time with my coffee, then got out and went for my morning walk to get some exercise. Just doing that, doing what I was in the habit of doing, helps get my morning off to a start. I'm thankful that I had developed good habits when I was feeling fine, because otherwise it would be hard to do those 'good for you' things when grief threatens to overwhelm you into not wanting to do anything."

And as quickly as the surge of emotion and vulnerability had risen, it ebbed with similar speed and we returned to Mark.

The Habit of Availability

Grandma continued with expounding Mark twelve. A theme of "habits" had naturally emerged as the Spirit made the Scriptures alive to us all.

"When the man did so much to set up the vineyard, he was putting everything into place to ensure its success and fruitfulness. He was planning for a harvest. Note here, it says he dug a *deep* winepress. Similarly, God is expecting much to come out of His Word being sent to us, and the gift of the Holy Spirit being in us.

"Every day, I just tell the Lord, 'Jesus, help me to be and do whatever You want me to do today.'

"Even though God expects fruitfulness from our lives, the great relief is, it's not up to us to produce it. He just wants our availability and if we have that posture towards Him, then the fruitfulness will come.

"Every day, when I ask the Lord to lead me into what He wants me to be and do that day, I am amazed at how he answers that simple little prayer! Almost every day He provides opportunities for fruitfulness, even at the 'slower' age of 92! Not a day goes by where someone doesn't call needing encouragement or prayer, and sometimes people just stop by for a chat and a visit, and of course, I have my Bible study groups that come to me. I don't even have to leave my house to have my vineyard bearing fruit and the winepress filling up. The Lord is just so gentle and good, to allow me to still be bearing fruit, even in this season of my life. It really is true—all he wants from us is willingness and availability. And He can take care of the rest."

"So later on, in the story when the owner of the vineyard sends a delegate to collect during the harvest, he's really not being harsh at all. Fruitfulness is just a byproduct of us allowing God access to the vineyard that was His to begin with. He just wants access to us and to our lives which can only happen to the extent that we are connected to Him."

The Habit of Reflection

After Grandma's seeming tangents, but maybe, rather, gold nuggets of wisdom and insight and examples from her life, we get back to the text. We'd only gone through two verses of the chapter so far.

*A man planted a vineyard. He put a wall around it, dug a pit for the winepress **and built a watchtower.** Mark 12:1*

"It's also interesting to note that the owner of the vineyard put a watchtower in place over the vineyard. A watchtower allows you to come up, above the nitty gritty of the farming in order to look over it all. A watchtower allows us to assess the work of our hands — to see a little bit ahead, and a little bit behind. I believe this reminds us to be alert to what God is doing — to sometimes lift our heads from what *we* are doing, in order to see what *He* is doing.

This is what journaling does for me. It is like a watchtower. I have journals and journals filled, and if I ever need a reminder of God's goodness or His power to speak to me in my circumstances, I can just pull one out and be reminded. With watchtower journaling, we can stop and climb the ladder to get an overview of our lives and record what God has done, or the ways He has blessed us or shown us things out of His Word. Then later we can look back and reflect on how good God has been in the past. Journaling can also be prayers: asking God for things to come in the future, desires of our hearts being laid out, and things that might otherwise worry us as we anticipate them. When we see them from the watchtower of journaling they lose their hold on us because we already gave them to the Lord. The habit of reflection, from being in the watchtower, and looking behind to see God's faithfulness in the past, causes us to look forward to the good things that He will do in the future. Then, as we climb back down from the watchtower and enter back into the vineyards, there can be peace and fulfillment as we tend to things there (quite possibly the tedious and rather mundane things you may have to set about doing each day).

A watchtower also allowed for a vineyard keeper to see if there is any danger approaching… thieves or storms that might be approaching that would damage the crops. When we reflect in light of God's Word, we can see if any sin is encroaching on our hearts. Not believing God's promises or disobeying what He tells us to do would definitely stunt fruitfulness, or even encroach on our families and those we are tending to. Reflecting is really just us being still and knowing that He is God and allowing him to speak to us about anything that might need the Holy Spirit's tending in our lives.

The Habit of Yielding

"Well, ladies, I know we're moving slowly through this, but it's just so rich, I don't want us to miss anything. I guess we can just plan on getting through this first parable today and we'll save the rest of Mark 12 for next week."

The ladies and I had hardly noticed. And we certainly weren't complaining.

We each had our journals open and were vigorously scribbling in them, attempting to capture every truth and every angle that poured out of the Scriptures when Anne read them. It amazed me that a passage I would have read through and summarized in five minutes, had become a forty-five-minute life lesson. When Grandma had read "*the Word of God is living and active, sharper than a two-edged sword, piercing to the division of soul and spirit,*" (Hebrews 4:12) she took literally the fact that every word in those first two verses was sharp, had meaning, and could speak into our lives.

We read on.

"At harvest time he sent a servant to the tenants to collect from them some of the fruit of the vineyard." Mark 12:2 (NIV)

"Ladies, I had already skipped ahead a little to that part when we were talking about the season of fruitfulness and harvest in our lives, so let's just continue…."

"But they seized him, beat him, and sent him away empty-handed. Then he sent another servant to them; they struck this man on the head and treated him shamefully. He sent still another, and that one they killed. He sent many others, some of them they beat, others they killed." Mark 12:3-5 (NIV)

"Remember how we were talking about habits? We can have habits that hold us up in hard times, or we can start to form habits that end up hurting us and disconnecting us from the Lord. This parable actually speaks to this.

"Note here, the owner wasn't being unreasonable to want a portion of the fruits of his vineyard that he had leased out. He was not being demanding, but rather very patient as he kept asking. He was enduring with the tenants' stubbornness and kept giving second chances and new opportunities for them to listen and respond. But for some reason the tenants did not recognize the owner's patience. They had forgotten their connectedness to the owner in this vineyard-leasing reciprocity. They weren't thankful for the use of the vineyard and weren't willing to yield what rightfully belonged to him. They stopped honoring him as the owner or submitting to his position."

"I think this is a good reminder of the command to *fear the Lord*. The Lord is so gentle and good and faithful and loving, but He is still to be feared. We won't respond to Him rightly unless He is honored as Lord and Master of this world and of our lives. A lack of reverence leads to the responses that we see"

"The tenants did not submit, and they refused to respect the messengers."

"The Lord has sent us a Messenger, the Holy Spirit, who speaks to us through the Bible and also through His gentle promptings. It is so important to listen when He speaks and to heed what He tells us to do."

"The tenants got in the habit of rejecting the messenger, so much so that when the master's own son came, they were so used to dismissing the messenger and continuing on in their own agenda that they even *killed him*. I know none of us would want to do this, but if we get in the habit of dismissing the Holy Spirit's promptings instead of yielding to them, then we might just become so closed off that we completely miss Jesus and reject Him out of our lives, like the tenants did when they killed the master's son."

"So. Watch your habits. Use the watchtower we talked about to evaluate what habits you are forming. Heed Paul's prompting in 1 Thessalonians 5:19 '*Do not quench the Spirit*' or, 'Don't put the Spirit's fire out in your life.' The more you listen to Him, the greater the fire will grow in you. The more you ignore Him, the more you put out His fire in your life. <u>He</u>… is the best habit. And He will lead you into forming habits that hold you."

~5~

A Message to Share

Grandma's presence in this world has changed it: raising five godly children, each of whom has impacted their spheres of influence in a myriad of ways; teaching alongside her husband in over 400 teaching missions throughout the US and the world; leading countless Sunday School classes and women's Bible studies instructing thousands; authoring and coauthoring multiple books.

Her impact has been widespread and significant.

But she hadn't *set out* to change the world.

On the contrary, she writes of herself in her book, <u>This I Know</u>:

"My innate shyness probably worsened during my teen years…. Without being conscious that I was doing it, I seemed to separate my life at home from my life at school or work. My shyness at times took the form of stoicism, indifference to both pain and pleasure…

"…God didn't give me any earth-shattering insights into what He was doing in my life at this time (I don't remember ever asking Him) but I do think He was trying to teach me that He is trustworthy, that I could depend on Him and that I had much to be grateful for (p. 13)."

Then, later in her life, after frequently moving from place to place with her husband, adding children into the family at each stop, being faithful in the mundane during their years at seminary, and then accepting the call to serve in small Episcopal congregations, she writes

"Charles quickly became well-known in the town for his lively piano playing and singing, and was a frequent speaker…

"…In the meantime, I was becoming almost as well known among the women…as someone who would listen to them and was discreet enough not to repeat their confidences. Without meaning to, I became in great demands as a "counselor"—a dispenser of sympathy, advice and prayers. My house was seldom empty, and my phone line was almost constantly in use" (p.51).

This was an apt description of her life when she was in her mid-forties, but half a century later, it also described her life in her nineties.

How did she go from an almost debilitating shyness in her teen years into impacting the world? How did the girl who struggled to have a conversation, even a pleasant one, in her teens turn into the confidante that everyone wanted to talk to? How did she go on to teach countless classes at churches and conferences, getting up in front of hundreds of people regularly, despite the fact that she would rather have been sitting in the back seat?

She walked humbly with her God.

She knew the trustworthiness of His character.

She drew deeply from the richness of His promises.

And others longed for what she had.

Anne Murphy had a message to share and the world *wanted* to hear it.

God, a Storyteller

I had oh-so-tactfully *threatened* my seven children into obediently staying in bed despite the fact that it was an hour before their normal bedtime. Of course, my stellar parenting tactic was justified because I needed to "call Grandma and find out what she wants you guys to know."

On this chilly February evening, I was ready with the very first question I had scribbled out on that scrap piece of paper when this "Heirloom writing project" descended upon me in that prayer time.

So, there I was, with children dispersed into their rooms pensively obeying and wondering how serious I was about the threat, and me locked in my bedroom with phone on speaker, paper and pen poised.

"So, Grandma, my first question for you is…

"What would you want the next generation of your family to know?"

"Well…"

And with passion and love and adoration she began speaking of the God she knew so intimately.

"God is so holy, and majestic and He's the Creator of each one of my family. He has a *plan* for each of them. But He doesn't *make* them walk in it. We have to listen to Him for it. **I want them to know just how close He is.** God has a purpose for each of their lives and I would want them to press into Him to know His purpose and plan. God gives it to us. I would just say, 'Don't miss it.'"

She continued with a story,

"I remember at one point we had a picture...I'm not sure where it is now, but it was a picture of Grandma Hunter's father's mother, that's my great-grandmother... if you didn't catch that. I never met her, but in the picture, she was sitting in a rocking chair and there was a Bible in her lap. I think that she must have read it a lot, especially if it was important enough to have in her lap in the picture. Anyways, the Bible is the one thing that can keep speaking to people throughout all the different generations. When you look at the Scriptures, it is not as much a book of how-tos but a book of stories. In them, God is always the initiator. He's telling His story. God's always working, always reaching out to His people, always trying to include them in His story. I want my family members to know that they get to be a part of His story, but they have to be ready to receive their roles.

"You know, when we are first born, we are born with clenched fists. As we grow, we begin to open our hands and learn to receive. I desire for each of my family members to just receive how *good* God is and accept His will and direction for their lives. We have to be childlike receivers, though. We need open hands to all He gives…. instead of clenched fists holding on to how *we* think our lives should go."

I'm furiously writing at this point, for she, unbeknownst to her, was diagnosing the exact source of the joyless malaise I had been experiencing in my motherhood. Raising seven kids with clenched fists as to how the day should go, what their behavior should be, or the speed at which the chores should get done is a miserable way to live. Childlike receiving, on the other hand, trusts the Giver, the Story Writer, and receives what is given with eager, open and grateful hands. She continued,

"Jesus is the Light of the world, and He lights our way. He can't help but light our path because He IS Light. When we sidle up next to Him, by reading what He speaks to us in the Scriptures, then we begin to see clearly our purpose and the part we are to play in His story.

"Prayer is also such a gift. Our whole family experienced this when the children were growing up. Donna came home from camp one year and shared about how they had prayed every night together in their cabins. She thought we should do that as a family, so we did. Each of the kids would pray about different things that were going on in their lives and that prayer time together facilitated the opportunity to *see* God's direct answers. One really specific time was when we were in seminary and our family was diligently praying every night about how we would pay a bill that was due. When God answered, He sent the exact amount we needed, and all the kids got to see how faithful and good God is!

"Another crucial part of being attentive to the Lord's purpose are quiet times. Having a habit of reading the Word and prayer becomes like a trellis on which the vine (of our lives) can grow. It has a structure to hold to and reach for, which leads to more and more growth. And when we're growing, we're also going to be bearing fruit. I guess that sort of goes back to being part of God's story. As we trust Him and grow in our closeness with Him, He'll make our lives fruitful and that will be fulfilling the purpose He has for each of us. God is a Storyteller, and He made us in His image. That means each of us, and each one of my children and grandchildren and great-grandchildren has a story to tell that will bring glory to Him.

"I was just reading Psalm 78 the other morning, about telling the next generation….
"Oh my people, hear my teaching…
I will open my mouth in parables.
I will utter hidden things, things from of old.
We will tell the next generation

The praiseworthy deeds of the Lord,
His power and the wonders He has done.
Psalm 78: 1,2,4 (NIV)"

And with that, because one can't really improve upon the very Scripture that Grandma was living out through these phone conversations, we called it a night. We said our goodbyes, and I thanked her for her time and for her wisdom and for just being *her*.

I knew that I would not be the only beneficiary of that night's conversation…. but as the message Grandma shared with me *changed me,* my kids would be the first to blessed by it.

A Message to Mothers

We sat on the patio, watching the purple pansies sway with the rush of the spring breeze.

"Grandma," I started to ask, "you raised a family of five during a time when often there were just two or three children in a home. Having raised a family in the 50s and now as you disciple young moms in the twenty-first century, what advice would you give to moms of this age?"

Without missing a beat, not even a pause to consider, she spoke the same words that God had spoken through David centuries before this modern 21st century.

"Be still and know that I am God."

"I see a lot of frenetic activity, frantic rushing in the moms of today. It's like there is a spirit of competition since everyone else is doing it, and there is the fear:

'If I don't rush around to keep up....

....my child will be left behind.'

"But, honey, *God* can do things for these kids that you can't do or even think to do. The Holy Spirit really will guide you if you'll be still enough to listen.

"God can enable you to do things that you didn't even think you could do. Slowing down to steep in God's Word can allow His heart to enter in you enough so that it flows out of you to your kids.

"Raising children, cherishing them and seeing the good in them is not meant to be rushed. If we rush them in the moments, we miss them-both the child *and* the moment. If we rush them into adult-like behavior we miss the fun of their young and growing years. Mothering often takes surrendering of one's own agenda- letting go of the standard, the way, or the time frame in which *we* think things should be done. Often we as adults expect children to act like adults. But we really need to get down on their level. Remember that children are children, and sometimes they just can't do things the way we might expect them to in order to meet our own convenience.

"I remember one instance which taught Granddaddy and me this lesson well. Granddaddy was in the living room sitting down in his armchair reading the newspaper. He asked Chris, who was only four or five at the time, to go get his glasses from the bedroom dresser. Chris returned empty-handed and said he couldn't find them. Granddaddy assured him that they were indeed there and encouraged him to go back and get them. Chris, again, returned empty-handed. Granddaddy told him once more to look a little harder. When, for the third time, Chris came back with no glasses, Granddaddy emerged from the armchair frustrated and went into the bedroom. Sure, enough they were sitting right there in plain view. About to reprimand Chris for not looking harder, a thought popped into his mind - it was probably the Holy Spirit (Grandma noted, as an aside). He got down on his knees, at the same eye level as his young son. At that angle, he saw from Chris's childlike point of view, and indeed the glasses were too far back on the dresser to be seen or even reached by the willing-but-incapable boy.

"Granddaddy told me the story when we were in bed that night, and it was such a good reminder for the both of us. It was as if God was admonishing us to go slow with our children and try to see things from their perspective.

"It reminded me of God being the Good Shepherd. A good shepherd checks in with each of his sheep daily for injuries, and thorns, and the like. He has to get down on their level and see if they are feeling any pain or needing any mending. Mothers need to be spending time with their Good Shepherd to pour out to Him any pain or worry they might have experienced, so that He can mend them. Then, with the comfort He gives them, they can extend it to their own children as they shepherd them. It's just what 2 Corinthians 1 says, '*God is our merciful Father and the source of all comfort. He comforts us in all our troubles so that we can comfort others*,' including our children. The more we do this with our own children, the healthier and more secure they will feel. You will have a happy and pleasant little flock!

"When we drive them too hard and don't really check in with them and bestow care on them, then we become like the shepherds that scattered the flock of God's people in Jeremiah 23, ' *"Woe to the shepherds who are destroying and scattering the sheep of My pasture!" declares the Lord."* ' I know that no mom would really want this, it's just that busyness sometimes creeps in. The wonderful news is that the Good Shepherd Himself promises to bring them back to their pasture and cause them to be fruitful and tend to them. Moms get the joy of participating in the tending of the children, their little sheep, along *with* Him."

Just Brag on Jesus

My husband and I were on a trip of a lifetime. Gifted an excursion to Norway without children, Danny and I were thrilled to be on an adventure together in the most beautiful and majestic of places. We were falling in love all over again—fourteen years, seven children and multiple ministry ventures after our initial romance began. I couldn't help but think of all the beautiful travel pictures of Grandma and Granddaddy posted around her home. *This* is why they led so many teaching mission groups on overseas trips. Traveling was absolutely wonderful.

There was only one problem.

We were going to have to go back.

Back to the intensity of our frantic schedules. Back to all the needs of seven kids. Back to the mountains of laundry, piles of dishes and scatterings of belongings throughout our home. But worst of all, we would be returning to my angry outbursts. These were always followed by shame, then remorse, apologies, and renewed resolve to love my kids well and be patient with them. I was so exhausted from the cycle of failure and defeat, and I was equally tired of *trying* so hard. All of my Bible studies and memorized verses and sermons about the gospel couldn't seem to penetrate this "thorn in my side."

We drove through the most breathtaking of landscapes.

And I just sobbed.

"I don't want to have to go back if I'm going to just keep screaming at the kids. I'm damaging them, and they just don't deserve it. I can't keep doing this!"

My attempting-to-be-helpful pastor-husband started sharing, "You're free. Jesus has set you free. There is no condemnation for those who are in Christ."

Upon hearing those words, deep emotion welled up…

I wanted to slap him.

"That's not helpful right now! Just pray in the Spirit, PLEASE!"

~~~~

I *knew t*he gospel, I *taught* people the gospel, but somehow "the gospel" knowledge wasn't enough to change my inner attitudes and outward actions.

I knew I needed a movement of the Spirit of God in my life to remove this continual "not good enough" mantra that plagued my head and heart. This continual inner mantra was often projected onto my children, my labors, and my life, always spoiling it all. It was also a mantra which Grandma often heard interwoven in our conversations together. Just a week before our trip to Norway, I had been sharing with Grandma the things that the Lord had been showing me from Galatians 5:3. "*I testify again to every [person] who accepts circumcision [or any type of law imposed on oneself to measure up to God's standard of "enough"], that he is obligated to keep the whole law.*"

"I can't pick and choose," I was telling her. "If I am depending on law at all, or trying to keep any part of it, instead of depending on Jesus, then the whole entire thing comes crashing down upon me. When I'm trusting in my performance or ability to keep it all together, I always end up falling flat on my face, which leads to despair…every time.

"You know, honey, it's actually a *good* thing that you end up flat on your face," Grandma had replied. "When we get to the end of ourselves we *have* to look to the Lord. It's a mercy, otherwise we would live under a false pretense that we don't really need the Lord as much as we do. When things are going well, we might actually even indulge the sneaking suspicion that we deserve to share some of His glory. But God very clearly says in His Word,

> *'I am the Lord. There is no other….*
> *I will not share My glory with another.'*
> *(Isaiah 42:8-11)*

"If God's goodness and faithfulness to us had anything to with our performance, then we would either get prideful or end up crushed with shame for not measuring up."

"Do you know what the way out is?"

I was eager to know how to get off this hamster wheel. My head knowledge sure wasn't helping.

"What's that, Grandma?"

"Brag on Jesus."

"Think about what *He* has done, not about what you have or haven't done. Speak about what He is doing. Talk about Him and His works. It takes the focus off of you, and with that it takes the pressure off.

"Honey, you've always been so hard on yourself and set impossible standards for yourself. It's *not* all up to you, it's really all about Him. Your salvation, the love God has for you, your faith, the way God might use you. It is all Him. So, talk about Him.

"Just keep bragging on Jesus."

~~~~

Danny did start praying during that drive. And as we drove through tunnels, mountains, valleys, and lush landscapes, the Spirit did a supernatural work.

A memory surfaced, one so vivid, from the young age of seven. In it, my best work had been criticized, and with the criticism a little lie, a thorn, was wedged into my tender heart.

The Holy Spirit descended on me, sobs came afresh, words came spilling out,

"I have to get it right! I have to get it right! I have to get it right!"

It was as if I was accessing for the first time a lie that had become so intertwined within all of my psyche, that it had pushed and pressured me all my life. "I have to get it right!" drove me as a young teen into an eating disorder, into overachieving academically, athletically, and spiritually (if that is even possible). It drove radical life choices, and perfectionistic parenting and unrealistic standards in all arenas of life, especially the standards I set for my children.

If, in all of life, one has to "get it right," then one is living for a moving target, striving for an achievement never quite achieved, aspiring toward a standard never quite reached.

As I wept, and as the tender Counselor pinpointed the exact issues in my heart, He also gave me a picture. A picture of Jesus Himself reaching in and removing this thorn which had been imbedded in me for so long. The thorn was the "I have to get it right!" lie. I suddenly realized why my husband's "gospel preaching" in the car had caused such a violent reaction in me. If a thorn is stuck in your foot, no amount of bandaging, padding, or pressing will bring comfort. Similarly, all the sermons listened to, Bible verses memorized, acts of charity performed only served to push the thorn of "I have to get it right" deeper. It only caused more pain and more pressure. I needed an outside source, a supernatural intervention, to *remove* the thorn, and *then* the gospel of Jesus saving sinners and of making all things right with the Father could be comforting. *Then* the sermons and the Scriptures and the prayers could be a restorative balm. The Great Physician had to remove the foreign object, and then His Word could bring healing into the wound.

Tears of relief now flowed, relief over having now realized what had kept me stuck for so long. Gratitude flooded me as I had just experienced the Holy Spirit's intimacy and an answer to my prayers to be changed. A new mantra filled my lips, one that surprisingly was the most freeing of words.

I. Won't. Get. It. Right.

I won't get it right.

But Jesus will.

Jesus did.

Jesus does…

And He has promised to do it (2 Peter 1:3; Acts 1:8) through His empowering Spirit.

~~~~

Grandma was right.

If He does it all,

then all I have to do is…

brag on Jesus.

~6~

Conclusion

"We're walking each other home."

-Anne Murphy
(April 2018)

It was the second morning after watching Grandma slip from the shell of this earthen vessel and into the Presence of the Most High where so many of my loved ones had already arrived. It was too emotionally difficult, too fresh and raw and overwhelming to be in her house—to start the morning with the Lord, opened Bible in lap and cup of coffee in hand—all without her there. Sterile Starbucks would have to serve as a makeshift "quiet time spot" that Birmingham morning. So instead of being surrounded by family pictures and the comfort of "Grandma's house familiarity," I sipped coffee and soaked in the Word there amongst nurses in scrubs, college kids with opened textbooks and older men studying the morning paper.

Grandma was not there, but the same Spirit that had lived in her was.

The Holy Spirit, whom Jesus promised would "lead you into all truth" (John 16:13) was doing for me what He had done for Grandma every morning for the past seven decades. The words began to pop, and the Scriptures began to come alive. The Spirit was taking the age-old message of the Bible along with my current situation and past experience to speak to me.

I had randomly opened to Psalm 107, and my eyes fell on verse 35...

"He turned desert into pools [streams] of water
And the parched ground into flowing springs;"
Psalm 107:35 (ESV)

Almost immediately I began underlining and jotting notes in my old, half-chewed-by-the-dog travel Bible. "Desert into streams of water" caught my eye, for a little book called *Streams in the Desert* [1], named directly from this verse, had been my lifeline after my mother passed away twenty years before. It had served as a trickling stream of hope in the midst of the desert of pain and loss and void. I had known the heat and thirst of living in the desert, a place lacking growth, a landscape dreary and unchanging, unable to naturally be a place where life could be cultivated.

Here, as I faced my second significant mother-loss, the future looked similarly bleak.

But God.

But God promises here to do the miraculous, the thing that goes against everything natural and expected in such a setting. He promises to turn the desert into a place of thirst-quench. He promises to take a parched place and cause potential for life and flourishing to well up from it.

Oh, glory! There *is* hope beyond Grandma in our lives. There is still nourishment to be had, maybe not on her floral couch chatting with her, but from the God who filled her and caused such life and richness to flow from her.

"There He brought the hungry to live,
and they founded a city where they could settle.
They sowed fields and planted vineyards
that yielded a fruitful harvest."
Psalm 107:36

"There."

There, right there, smack dab in the middle of the desert. That is where they settled; and not only settled, but founded a city, and sowed fields, and planted vineyards, and reaped a fruitful harvest.

Am I willing to truly settle wherever the Lord leads me? Even if it is in the midst of a desert of grief and loss? Do I believe enough in the Wellspring of Life, Jesus Christ, that there could be life to be found and flourishing *anywhere* (Acts 17:28; John 4:14)? After all, Jesus claimed that He *is* the life and promised to never leave us or forsake us (John 14:6; Hebrews 13:5)

"I am the Bread of Life" (John 6:35), In [Christ], all things live and move and have their being. (Acts 17:28)

Grandma's life was a testimony of the flourishing and fruitfulness of settling in barren places. She didn't have an idyllic life void of suffering and deserts, but she managed to settle and flourish in whatever landscape she found herself. Whether that be as a 10-year-old with her father dead and her mother desperately struggling to make ends meet. Or as a preteen with family crammed into an upstairs apartment, yielding what had once been the spacious family home to renters. Or while moving from place to place following her young husband's dream of "making it" in show business. Or during her time of raising a large family during a career shift and seminary and then ministry. Or when functioning as "resident life counselor" to the masses as she served as the "rector's wife" for so many years in so many different small parishes. Or in the midst of walking through grief after grief of losing mother, then daughter, then husband. Or when learning to live as a widow and create a life apart from the one with whom she had been one flesh for more than half a century. Or in her last few years, while still ministering to her local church, to the various women who graced her home for multiple weekly Bible studies, and to the numerous children, grandchildren and great-grandchildren who came for Grandma visits. Or, more recently, in losing her son and beloved brother. No matter what the season, there was flourishing.

She had found the secret of the streams that well up in the desert:

He.

He turned.

He turned the desert into streams of water. (Ps. 107:35)

Grandma knew that God was able. God was willing. God was good.

He was how flourishing could be found anywhere.

So, she followed Him and settled and sowed and planted,

He blessed [her] and [her] numbers greatly increase,
and He did not let [her] herds diminish…
He lifted the needy out of [her] affliction
and increased [her] families like flocks.
Psalm 107: 38,41 (NIV)

My own life is a manifestation of God's promise-keeping to Grandma, and to her "increased families." The very reason I have been privileged to have strong support, wise counsel, continual encouragement and faithful prayers is because of *Grandma's* flourishing. Her continual drinking of the Living Water, no matter where she was, provided rivers of living water flowing from within her, streams that nourished and refreshed many who found themselves in deserts (John 7:38). It has caused a trickle effect of flourishing in my own walk with Christ, my own faith endeavors, and my own ministry, marriage and family. Many more can claim the same. Without Grandma "here" it might be easy to melt into despondency over "all being lost." But the same Living Water that nourished her and then refreshed others is available to us who mourn her loss and to those who did not even know her until reading of her now. We all have griefs we bear. But the same comfort she received, the same Scriptures that spoke clearly, the same Spirit who empowered are all accessible to each one of us.

God the Father planned a direct access for *all* of us — by sending His Son Jesus *amongst* us, to walk righteously *on behalf of* us, to pay for wrongdoing *instead* of us, and to rise from death *ahead* of us. Then Jesus' ascension to the Father enabled an empowerment *within* us. Grandma has passed from this temporal life, but God's faithfulness, His Word, and His Spirit have not. We have the opportunity now to believe, to trust, and to walk and commune with the Lord the way she did. And we have the opportunity and privilege to do it alongside each other.

We are walking each other home. Grandma has simply arrived there ahead of us.

> *The upright see and rejoice…*
> *Whoever is wise, let him heed these things*
> *and consider the great love of the Lord.*

> *Psalm 107:42-43 (NIV)*

[1]Cowman, L.B. **Streams in the Desert.** Grand Rapids: Zondervan, 1997.

About the Author

Kimberly A. Iverson is a pastor's wife and urban missionary. She lives with her husband, Danny, and their seven (soon to be eight) children in Atlanta, Georgia. She homeschools, runs road races with her son, reads a loud (a lot), leads discipleship groups in her neighborhood, and totes children (both her own and plenty of extras) to various and sundry activities. She is also the proud granddaughter of the late Anne Murphy. She blogs at www.journeytoshalom.com and instagrams @kimberlyaiverson

Made in the USA
Middletown, DE
11 November 2019